US MILITARY

AIR COMMANDOS

BY CHARLES MARLIN

Apex is distributed by North Star Editions:
sales@northstareditions.com | 888-417-0195

Produced for Apex by Red Line Editorial.

Photographs ©: Joe Giddens/PA Images/Getty Images, cover; Senior Airman Miranda Mahoney/US Air Force/DVIDS, 1, 24–25; Trevor Cokley/US Air Force/DVIDS, 4–5; Capt. Jessica Tait/US Air Force/DVIDS, 6; Sgt. Michael Knight/US Army/DVIDS, 7; Airman 1st Class Gracelyn Hess/US Air Force/DVIDS, 8–9; DVIDS, 10–11; iStockphoto, 12–13, 20, 29; Tech. Sgt. Shawn Nickel/US Air Force/DVIDS, 14–15; Airman Samantha Rossi/US Air Force/DVIDS, 16–17; Senior Airman Jeff Parkinson/US Air Force, 18; Airman 1st Class Dillon Johnston/US Air Force/DVIDS, 19; 2nd Lt. Merit Davey/US Air Force/DVIDS, 21; Airman 1st Class Caleb Pavao/US Air Force/DVIDS, 22–23; Airman 1st Class Kyla Gifford/US Air Force/DVIDS, 24; US Army/DVIDS, 26; Tech. Sgt. Carly Kavish/US Air Force/DVIDS, 27

Library of Congress Control Number: 2025939210

ISBN
979-8-89250-802-5 (hardcover)
979-8-89250-831-5 (paperback)
979-8-89250-886-5 (ebook pdf)
979-8-89250-860-5 (hosted ebook)

Printed in the United States of America
Mankato, MN
012026

NOTE TO PARENTS AND EDUCATORS

Apex books are designed to build literacy skills in striving readers. Exciting, high-interest content attracts and holds readers' attention. The text is carefully leveled to allow students to achieve success quickly. Additional features, such as bolded glossary words for difficult terms, help build comprehension.

TABLE OF CONTENTS

CHAPTER 1

RESCUE FROM ABOVE

Gunfire booms, and bullets fly. A V-22 Osprey zips through the air. An Air Commando is its pilot. She hovers over the battle.

Air Commandos often carry soldiers and supplies to and from battles.

Medics in the Air Force help give care on the ground or during flights.

A hurt soldier lies on the ground. The pilot lands near him. A **medic** sprints out. He bandages a deep cut on the man's leg. Then he loads the soldier onto the aircraft.

AMAZING AIRCRAFT

The V-22 Osprey has **propellers**. They can face upward. That helps the aircraft move like a helicopter. Or the propellers can face forward. Then the aircraft can fly like a plane.

Like a helicopter, a V-22 Osprey can take off or land without a runway.

The pilot quickly takes off. She dives and swerves to avoid enemy fire. The Osprey speeds to a nearby hospital.

A V-22 Osprey can carry more than 30 people.

FAST FACT

The V-22 Osprey has a top speed of 315 miles per hour (507 km/h).

CHAPTER 2

AIR COMMANDO HISTORY

The Air Commandos are part of the US Air Force. They formed during World War II (1939–1945). Commandos helped British troops. They provided air support.

General Henry H. Arnold founded the Air Commandos in 1944.

After the war, the Air Commandos split up. Later, the United States began facing new types of enemies. Some were **guerrillas**. In 1962, the Commandos restarted. They helped fight back.

SPREADING FEAR

Air Commandos fought in the Vietnam War (1954–1975). They flew over Vietnamese towns. Speakers blasted **propaganda** messages. Aircraft dropped papers with propaganda, too. Many enemy soldiers gave up.

Some Air Commandos flew C-47 Skytrains during the Vietnam War.

Today, the group carries out missions all over the world. It fights against **terrorists**. And it helps take down **dictators**.

FAST FACT

Air Commandos may help after disasters. They travel to places hit by fires, earthquakes, or storms.

In 2017, hurricanes hit islands in the Caribbean Sea. Air Commandos brought supplies such as food and water.

CHAPTER 3

TOUGH TRAINING

Soldiers get special training to become Air Commandos. First, they take classes. They learn about different types of fighting. They also study languages and **cultures**.

Air Commandos take courses at Hurlburt Field in Florida.

Soldiers do a field-skills course next. They train to use weapons. They learn to fly planes and other vehicles. They also learn to treat injuries.

Air Commando vehicles may have armor. These hard coverings help keep vehicles safe.

Air Commandos may practice water rescues.

AIRDROPS

Commandos often do airdrops. They leap from flying planes. They **parachute** down to the ground. Sometimes, they land in water. They may do missions at night.

Air Commandos learn how to find threats such as hidden bombs.

Commandos learn to identify threats. They plan ways to avoid problems. For example, they learn to negotiate. They try to talk with people before using force.

FAST FACT

Commando training is intense. Up to 90 percent of soldiers may drop out before training is done.

Staying fit helps Air Commandos carry out tough missions.

CHAPTER 4

ALWAYS READY

Air Commandos must be ready for missions at any time. They train every day. They work out and practice fighting.

Air Commandos use many types of weapons

Night vision goggles help people see in low light. They also make things look green.

Commandos also carry lots of gear. Their packs are filled with survival supplies. They use radios. And their helmets often have night vision goggles.

GHOSTRIDERS

Air Commandos may fly AC-130J Ghostriders. These planes carry several types of guns and missiles. And they can spot targets from nearly 10 miles (16 km) away.

An AC-130J Ghostrider can fly about 3,000 miles (4,800 km) before needing more fuel.

In 2003, the Air Commandos worked with the Green Berets in Iraq.

Commandos sometimes team up with other soldiers, such as the US Army's Green Berets. Commandos can help with attacks from above. Or they may spy on enemies.

Air Commandos sometimes use powerful MQ-9 Reaper drones.

FAST FACT

Some Commandos use **drones**. The drones fly over enemy areas and track targets.

COMPREHENSION QUESTIONS

Write your answers on a separate piece of paper.

1. Write a few sentences explaining the main ideas of Chapter 3.

2. What do you think would be the hardest part of becoming an Air Commando? Why?

3. What training do Air Commandos complete first?

A. taking classes
B. using weapons
C. learning to fly planes

4. Why do Air Commandos carry lots of gear?

A. so they can move faster
B. so they are ready for many challenges
C. so they don't have to fly planes

5. What does **support** mean in this book?

They helped British troops. They provided air ***support****.*

A. tests
B. problems
C. help

6. What does **intense** mean in this book?

Commando training is ***intense****. Up to 90 percent of soldiers may drop out before training is done.*

A. hard
B. fast
C. easy

Answer key on page 32.

GLOSSARY

cultures

Groups of people and the ways they live, including their beliefs and laws.

dictators

Leaders with total power, especially those who are cruel.

drones

Aircraft that people control from far away.

guerrillas

Fighters who use surprise attacks.

medic

A soldier who gives emergency medical care.

parachute

To jump from high up while wearing fabric to slow one's fall.

propaganda

Messages that try to make people do or think certain things.

propellers

Spinning blades that make vehicles go.

terrorists

People who attack and scare others to reach their goals.

TO LEARN MORE

BOOKS

Gaertner, Meg. *US Air Force*. Apex Editions, 2023.

Hamilton, John. *United States Air Force*. Abdo Publishing, 2021.

Marlin, Charles. *Helicopters*. Apex Editions, 2025.

ONLINE RESOURCES

Visit **www.apexeditions.com** to find links and resources related to this title.

ABOUT THE AUTHOR

Charles Marlin is an author, editor, and avid cyclist. He lives in rural Iowa.

INDEX

ANSWER KEY:
1. Answers will vary; 2. Answers will vary; 3. A; 4. B; 5. C; 6. A